The
QUOTABLE
DAD

Appreciation from the Greatest Minds in History

Copyright © 2013 by Familius

Published by Familius LLC, www.familius.com

Familius books are available at special discounts for bulk purchases for sales promotions, family or corporate use. Special editions, including personalized covers, excerpts of existing books, or books with corporate logos, can be created in large quantities for special needs. For more information, contact Premium Sales at 559-876-2170 or email specialmarkets@familius.com

Library of Congress Catalog-in-Publication Data

2014935257

pISBN 978-1-938301-46-9
eISBN 978-1-938301-68-1

Printed in the United States of America

Edited by Brooke Jorden, Emily Smith, and Aven Rose
Cover Design by David Miles
Book design by Maggie Wickes

10 9 8 7 6 5 4 3 2 1

First Edition

TABLE OF CONTENTS

FATHERHOOD AND RELATIONSHIPS

"Blessed indeed is the man who hears many gentle voices call him 'Father'!"

—Lydia M. Child, *Philothea: A Romance*

Fatherhood is a sacred role. One of the most meaningful relationships we will form in life is with our father or father-figure. You'll always remember the times Dad embarrassed you in front of your friends. You'll always remember the times he bought your mother flowers or held her hand. And you'll always remember the time he spent teaching you to ride a bike or catch a fish or flip an omelet. The relationship a father has with his children is precious and unique, and even more than that, necessary. Loving, attentive fathers raise happier, more well-adjusted children because those children have a positive role model to learn from and lean on. Involved fathers raise more responsible children. Sons are better behaved and daughters have better self-esteem when they have a good relationship with their father. It's just a fact.

While the relationship between a mother and child is immediate and physical, not to mention emotional, a father's relationship with his children takes a little extra effort. This relationship requires nothing more than the basics: time and love. It's a simple equation, but all too often one aspect or the other is neglected. However, when both ingredients are given in generous measure, fathers can build a relationship with their children that will stand the tests of time, trial, and temper.

Like any relationship, the father-child relationship will grow and change with time. When children are little, their father is their hero. He is the smartest, the strongest, the coolest man in the world, and children will do anything to make him proud. For a teenager, Dad may be old-fashioned and pushy, but he will always be there when you need him. When children become adults, they look back on the wit and wisdom of their fathers and see that all of his actions—mistakes included—were motivated by love. Our relationship with our fathers may even change as we see his relationships and interactions with others—with his wife, with his parents, with your siblings, and with your own spouse and children.

Embarking on parenthood is a daunting task, but every father knows the beautiful feeling of holding a child for the first time and knowing that all he wants to do is love and protect it. That simplistic relationship will grow as the child grows, and as children grow, parents do too. Fathers will discover surprising new characteristics about themselves and experience feelings that they never knew existed. Fatherhood is nothing more than transformation by love.

These quotes express the joys of fatherhood and the unique relationship that exists between a father and his children.

—*Brooke Jorden*

"There is nothing that moves a loving father's soul quite like his child's cry."

—Joni Eareckson Tada
Author and radio personality

"We never know the love of a parent till we become parents ourselves."

—Henry Ward Beecher
American clergyman and social reformer

"I cannot think of any need in childhood as strong as the need for a father's protection."

—Sigmund Freud
Austrian neurologist and psychoanalyst

"Until you have a son of your own, you will never know the joy, the love beyond feeling that resonates in the heart of a father as he looks upon his son. You will never know the sense of honor that makes a man want to be more than he is and to pass something good and hopeful into the hands of his son. And you will never know the heartbreak of the fathers who are haunted by the personal demons that keep them from being the men they want their sons to be."

—Kent Nerburn
American author, sculptor, and educator

"An almost perfect relationship with his father was the earthly root of all his wisdom. From his own father, he said, he first learned that fatherhood must be at the core of the universe."

— C.S. Lewis
Writer, *Phantastes*

"The surprising thing about fatherhood was finding my inner mush. Now I want to share it with the world."

—Christopher Meloni
American actor

"The most important thing a father can do for his children is to love their mother."

—Theodore Hesburgh
American educator and former president of the University of Notre Dame

"What I love most about fatherhood is the opportunity to be a part of the development process of a new life."

—Seal
British R&B singer-songwriter

"The joys of parents are secret, and so are their griefs and fears."

—Sir Francis Bacon
English philosopher, statesman, and scientist

I watch the faces of single people in their twenties after I bring up that I "have children."

I imagine them taking a small step backward as if to avoid contagion, with a look of "Sorry to hear that" on their face.

Like I naively volunteered to contract leprosy, forever quarantining myself from the world of having fun by having children.

Well, why not?

I guess the reasons against having more children always seem uninspiring and superficial.

What exactly am I missing out on? Money? A few more hours of sleep? A more peaceful meals? More hair?

These are nothing compared to what I get from these five monsters who rule my life. I believe each of my five children has made me a better man.

So I figure I only need another thirty-four kids to be a pretty decent guy. Each one of them has been a pump of light into my shriveled black heart. I would trade money, sleep, or hair for a smile from one of my children in a heartbeat.

Well, it depends on how much hair.

—Jim Gaffigan
American comedian and author

A Father's Love

A father is

respected
because he gives his children
leadership,

appreciated
because he gives his children
care,

valued
because he gives his children
time,

loved
because he gives his children the
one thing they treasure most—
himself.

—Anonymous

"Watching your husband become a father is really sexy and wonderful."

—Cindy Crawford
American model

"Father!—to God himself we cannot give a holier name."

—William Wordsworth
English Romantic poet

"When you get pure joy out of 'being' rather than 'doing' or 'seeing,' that's when you realize how big and unexplainable some things are, and being a dad is one of those very few things."

—Brendan Fehr
Canadian actor

"I have to be careful not to let the world dazzle me so much that I forget that I'm a husband and a father."

—Herbie Hancock
American musician and composer

"The most important things in my father's life? World peace. Me and my brother. My mom."

—Sean Lennon
American musician and son of John Lennon

7

"I met my grandfather just before he died, and it was the first time that I had seen Dad with a relative of his. It was interesting to see my own father as a son and the body language and alteration in attitude that comes with that, and it sort of changed our relationship for the better."

—Christian Bale
English actor

"The heart of a father is the masterpiece of nature."

— Antoine François Prévost
Manon Lescaut

"What makes you a man is not the ability to have a child. It's the courage to raise one."

—Barack Obama
44th US president

"I am not ashamed to say that no man I ever met was my father's equal, and I never loved any other man as much."

—Hedy Lamarr
Austrian-American actress and inventor

"A father is someone who carries pictures where his money used to be."

—Anonymous

**Creating a child
takes no love or skill;
being a parent
requires
lots of both.**

—Michael Josephson
American author and ethicist

It is a wise father that knows his own child.

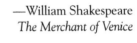

—William Shakespeare
The Merchant of Venice

"No one was more important than my mom and dad. I know they are watching from a place up in heaven here today to make sure all their kids are doing good."

—Eddie Murray
American MLB baseball player

"The military infrastructure grew me. My faith in God is important, my belief in my country is important, my relationship to my family is important, the things that Mom and Dad tell you growing up are important."

—Tommy Franks
retired US Army General

"I would have to say the person with whom I am most in love is definitely my son, Everly Bear. Although I'm his dad, I'm also his friend."

—Anthony Kiedis
American singer-songwriter

"Fatherhood will put a man through a lot, but it's a tremendous job, the best in the world—even better than playing basketball."

—Derek Fisher
American NBA basketball player

"It is a wise father who knows his child. But maybe it's a very wise child who takes time to know his father."

—Anonymous

"No man can possibly know what life means, what the world means, until he has a child and loves it. And then the whole universe changes and nothing will ever again seem exactly as it seemed before."

—Lafcadio Hearn
international writer

"No word makes me happier than the word 'daddy' when it's directed to me."

—Michael Josephson
American author and ethicist

"Few sons are like their fathers—many are worse, few better."

—Homer
The Odyssey

"Parents are often so busy with the physical rearing of children that they miss the glory of parenthood, just as the grandeur of the trees is lost when raking leaves."

—Marcelene Cox
American writer

The father who would taste the **essence** of his fatherhood must turn back from ● the plane of his **experience,** take with him the fruits of his journey, and begin again beside his child, marching step by step over the same old road.

—Angelo Patri
Italian-American
author and educator

"You will find that if you really try to be a father, your child will meet you halfway."

—Robert Brault
American operatic tenor

"It is not flesh and blood but the heart which makes us fathers and sons."

—Friedrich Schiller
German poet and philosopher

HUMOR
AND LIFE

"By the time a man realizes that maybe his father
was right, he usually has a son who thinks he's
wrong."

—Charles Wadsworth, American classical pianist

When the first baby laughed for the first time . . . she was
probably laughing at her dad. From the funny faces to the
awful jokes to the hideous sweaters they just won't get rid
of, dads always have a way of making us laugh. Fatherhood
requires the kind of sense of humor that is humble, but not
self-deprecating; silly, but not dismissive; and playful, but
not hurtful. Fathers need to be able to laugh at their children's antics, at their own weaknesses, and at life's general
ups and downs.

The inevitable joy of fatherhood comes in finding the
humor in your children. All fathers carry enormous responsibilities, but even when it's been a rough day at work, there
are still scoldings to give and messes to clean up when they
get home. However, when a father can see the humor in his
children's actions, his positivity can demonstrate his love

for his children. Dad can be the guy who chuckles rather than yells—although the latter may often be more tempting. Many children develop long-standing jokes with their fathers that they carry with them into adulthood, and these shared experiences solidify the bond between a child and his or her father, giving the child a loving memory to hold onto even after the father is gone.

Fathers can always find humor in their own shortcomings. Like many long-term occupations, fatherhood is a learn-on-the-job gig, and fathers are bound to make some mistakes. But being able to laugh at what you thought you knew is both healthy and constructive. And as any father knows, if you have a hard time seeing your own failings, your children will surely point out some weaknesses for you to laugh at.

Sometimes life can be difficult. Life happens. From financial problems to struggling children to marital stress, a father could easily get bogged down in the day to day drudge. But a good laugh is a cure-all remedy—both mentally and physically. Humor won't make problems disappear, but a sense of humor can equip a father to boldly face the trying times that come to every family.

These quotes demonstrate the power of humor in dealing with the struggles—and the joys—of fatherhood.

—*Brooke Jorden*

"Children are a great comfort in your old age—and they help you reach it faster, too."

—Lionel Kauffman
American author

"I want my son to wear a helmet twenty-four hours a day."

—Will Arnett
Canadian actor

"A new father quickly learns that his child invariably comes to the bathroom at precisely the times when he's in there, as if he needed company."

—Bill Cosby
American actor and comedian

"My dad taught me true words you have to use in every relationship: 'Yes, baby.'"

—Star Jones
American lawyer, writer, and TV personality

"My kids love it. I thought I was the coolest dad in the world when I got to be in a Bond film, but *Harry Potter*, too? Well, I think I qualify for a medal for exceptional parenting or something, don't you?"

—Robbie Coltrane
Scottish actor and comedian

Insanity
is hereditary;
you get it from
your children.

Sam Levenson
American writer and comedian

"Whoever does not have a good father should procure one."

—Friedrich Nietzsche
German philosopher and critic

"Fatherhood is great because you can ruin someone from scratch."

—Jon Stewart
American political satirist and TV show host

"For Father's Day, my kids always give me a bottle of cologne called English Leather. It's appropriate! To them I always smell like a wallet."

—Robert Orben
American writer and humorist

"When I was about twelve and first started wearing lipstick, my dad would ask, 'Are you wearing makeup?' I would say back, 'You're wearing more makeup there than I am!'"

—Georgia Jagger
Model and daughter of Rolling Stones lead singer, Mick Jagger

"Having a staring contest with a newborn is one of the weirdest things you will ever do. And it is highly recommended."

—Ross McCammon
American author and editor

"There should be a children's song: 'If you're happy and you know it, keep it to yourself and let your dad sleep.'"

—Jim Gaffigan
American comedian and author

"There are three stages of a man's life: he believes in Santa Claus, he doesn't believe in Santa Claus, he is Santa Claus."

—Bob Phillips
American television journalist

"When I was a boy of fourteen, my father was so ignorant I could hardly stand to have the old man around. But when I got to be twenty-one, I was astonished at how much he had learned in seven years."

—Mark Twain
American author and satirist

"Never raise your hand to your kids. It leaves your groin unprotected."

—Red Buttons
American actor and comedian

"The father is always a Republican toward his son, and his mother's always a Democrat."

—Robert Frost
American poet

If the new American father feels bewildered and even defeated, let him take comfort from the fact that whatever he does in any fathering situation has a fifty percent chance of being right.

—Bill Cosby
American actor and comedian

FATHERHOOD
is pretending
the present you
love most is
SOAP-ON-A-ROPE.

—Bill Cosby
American actor and comedian

"Becoming a father is easy enough, but being one can be very rough."

—Wilhelm Busch
German poet, artist, and humorist

"It would seem that something which means poverty, disorder, and violence every single day should be avoided entirely, but the desire to beget children is a natural urge."

—Phyllis Diller
American actress and comedian

"My wife is so analytical with raising kids, and I am not. My feeling is if they turn out good, then that means I was a good daddy and put a lot of effort into it. If they turn out bad, it means they took after her side of the family."

—Jeff Foxworthy
American comedian and outdoorsman

"My dad, like many Southern men, is this very emotionally expressive person who isn't as articulate in words about his feelings as he is with breaking a chair or something like that."

—Lucy Alibar
American screenwriter

"My father hated radio, and he could not wait for television to be invented so that he could hate that, too."

–Peter De Vries
American editor and novelist

"My father used to play with my brother and me in the yard. Mother would come out and say, 'You're tearing up the grass.' 'We're not raising grass,' Dad would reply. 'We're raising boys.'"

—Harmon Killebrew
American Major League baseball player

"I kept my babies fed. I could have dumped them, but I didn't. I decided that whatever trip I was on, they were going with me. You're looking at a real daddy."

—Barry White
American composer and singer-songwriter

"I try to be hard-boiled sometimes. My kids see right through it. I'm acting. It's always, 'When I say you'll be back at 11:00, that means 11:00, not 11:15. Do you hear me?!' Then, 'Yeah, Dad.' Of course, he'll come back at midnight or 12:30."

—Liam Neeson
Irish actor

The thing about   having a bunch of
kids
is that you end up doing
once-in-a-lifetime
things
more than
once in a lifetime.

—Jim Gaffigan
American comedian and author

"I cannot understand how I managed to cope without getting cuddled this many times a day."

—Russell Crowe
New Zealand–born actor and producer

"Why are men reluctant to become fathers? They aren't through being children."

—Cindy Garner
American actress

"My father taught me to work, but not to love it. I never did like to work, and I don't deny it. I'd rather read, tell stories, crack jokes, talk, laugh—anything but work."

—Abraham Lincoln
16th US President

"My dad came over to the house, went into his pocket, and pulled out a handful of money, and began to pass it out to the children. This was the same man who, when I was his child, I would ask him for fifty cents, this man would tell me his life's story."

—Bill Cosby
American actor and comedian

Spread the diaper in the position of the diamond with you at bat. Then fold second base down to home, and set the baby on the pitcher's mound. Put first base and third together, bring up home plate, and pin the three together. Of course, in case of rain, you gotta call the game and start all over again.

—Jimmy Piersall
American Major League baseball player

PERSEVERANCE

"Being a great father is like shaving. No matter how well you shaved today, you have to do it again tomorrow."

—Reed Markham, American author and professor

In ancient Greece, the soldier Pheidippides fought with the outnumbered Athenian army against the Persians, who attacked the Greek city of Marathon. When the Athenians achieved victory over the Persians, Pheidippides ran approximately twenty-five miles from Marathon to Athens to deliver the news. According to legend, when he arrived at Athens, he declared "*Niki!*" (or "Victory!") and then fell down dead. The marathon we know today commemorates Pheidippides's sacrifice.

At first glance, the story of Pheidippides is tragic. However, in a metaphorical sense, Pheidippides's experience is extremely relatable. Life is like a marathon—not a short sprint—and fatherhood is no different. Each mile is an achievement, but there are always more to come, and we can't cut corners. So, amidst the daily difficulties with very few visible rewards in the interim, how do fathers keep on running? In the end, the answer is the same in the literal and metaphorical sense: pace yourself and keep your goal in mind.

While most of us believe we could never run an entire marathon—a whopping 26.2 miles—the human body is perfectly capable of running even farther when fueled by proper conditioning and determination. Perseverance is simply teaching yourself that you can handle more than you thought you could—physically and emotionally. Fathers know this principle better than most, and the best fathers instill that mindset in their children. The best fathers push their children to do difficult things in order to prepare them for a difficult world.

Many fathers teach their children perseverance by example. No matter how many times Dad takes out the trash, it always fills up again. No matter how many days Dad gets up and goes to work, he'll still have to go to work again come Monday. No matter how many times he pays the bills, he'll still have to pay them again next month. The marathon of life marches on, and so does he.

Fatherhood is not for the faint of heart. Fathers must persevere because the daily job of being a father doesn't end until the race of life is over—and maybe not even then. That isn't to say that fatherhood is a chore. On the contrary, fatherhood often brings with it great joy and satisfaction. True perseverance simply means harnessing those happy memories to help you push through the hard times. The trick to fatherhood is not merely enduring it, but enjoying it, and knowing that the end goal is victory for your family. Just keep running!

These quotes express the value—and ultimate rewards—of perseverance.

—*Brooke Jorden*

"From my dad, I learned to be good to people, to always be honest and straightforward. I learned hard work and perseverance."

—Luke Bryan
American country singer

"Perseverance is the hard work you do after you get tired of doing the hard work you already did."

—Newt Gingrich
American politician

"I think I got my business notions and my sense for that sort of thing from my dad. My dad never had a chance to go to school. He couldn't read and write. But he was so smart. He was just one of those people that could just make the most of anything and everything that he had to work with."

—Dolly Parton
American singer-songwriter and actress

"I inherited that calm from my father, who was a farmer. You sow, you wait for good or bad weather, you harvest, but working is something you always need to do."

—Miguel Indurain
Spanish road racing cyclist

"I am not a father who wants to give his kids everything. They have to earn it."

—Mariano Rivera
Panamanian MLB baseball player

"In the realm of ideas, everything depends on enthusiasm ... in the real world, all rests on perseverance."

—Johann Wolfgang von Goethe
German writer and politician

"I think one of the most important attributes is perseverance."

—David Rose
American composer and conductor

"I've had a hard life, but my hardships are nothing against the hardships that my father went through in order to get me to where I started."

—Bartrand Hubbard

"As Daddy said, life is ninety-five percent anticipation."

—Gloria Swanson
American actress, singer, and producer

"Perseverance, secret of all triumphs."

—Victor Hugo
French novelist and poet

**Becoming a father,
I think it inevitably
changes your**
perspective **on life.
I don't get nearly enough sleep.
And the simplest things
in life are**
completely satisfying.

—Hugh Jackman
Australian actor and producer

Perseverance

is a great element of success.
If you only
knock long enough
and loud enough at the gate,
you are sure to wake up
somebody.

—Henry Wadsworth Longfellow
American poet and educator

"My dad is like a cactus—introverted and tough. I'm a people person, like my mom, but I got my competitiveness from my dad. He came to this country from Belarus with nothing and built a real business. He's my hero for giving me that need to run a business and for having enormous confidence in me."

—Gary Vaynerchuk
CEO and entrepreneur

"It's hard having kids because it's boring . . . It's just being with them on the floor while they be children. They read *Clifford the Big Red Dog* to you at a rate of fifty minutes a page, and you have to sit there and be horribly proud and bored at the same time."

—Louis C.K.
Mexican-American comedian, writer, and actor

"I think the hardest thing about making music now is being a great dad at the same time. There's an insanity that goes with writing—a mad scientist thing that you have to go through—and sacrificing a kid's upbringing to do that is not an option."

—Eddie Vedder
American musician and singer-songwriter

"Hard work spotlights the character of people: some turn up their sleeves, some turn up their noses, and some don't turn up at all."

—Sam Ewing
American MLB baseball player

"Football is like life—it requires perseverance, self-denial, hard work, sacrifice, dedication, and respect for authority."

—Vince Lombardi
American football player and coach

"I do not think that there is any other quality so essential to success of any kind as the quality of perseverance. It overcomes almost everything, even nature."

—John D. Rockefeller
American oil tycoon and philanthropist

"I'm not sure what the future holds, but I do know that I'm going to be positive and not wake up feeling desperate. As my dad said 'Nic, it is what it is, it's not what it should have been, not what it could have been, it is what it is.'"

—Nicole Kidman
Australian actress, singer, and producer

The
three great essentials
to achieve anything
WORTHWHILE
are
HARD WORK,
stick—to—itiveness,
and
common sense.

—Thomas A. Edison
American inventor and businessman

My father taught me that the only way you can make good at anything is to **practice**, and then **practice** some more.

—Pete Rose
MLB baseball player and manager

"My dad has always been really helpful. He taught me that talent is a bonus, but persistence is what wins out."

—Zosia Mamet
American actress

"Men fail much oftener from want of perseverance than from want of talent."

—William Cobbett
English journalist and reformer

"Henry James once defined life as that predicament which precedes death, and certainly nobody owes you a debt of honor or gratitude for getting him into that predicament. But a child does owe his father a debt, if Dad, having gotten him into this peck of trouble, takes off his coat and buckles down to the job of showing his son how best to crash through it."

—Clarence B. Kelland
American writer

SUCCESS

"A father, finding time for what is most important, is the true marker of a successful person."

—Rick Warren, American pastor and author

History shows us "a man's world." Men build towers, bridges, businesses, and nations. Their success is measured by their power or influence or wealth. And yet, from the conqueror to the corporate tycoon, no man's endeavor has ever been as lasting, no success as meaningful, no expedition as perilous, as fatherhood. Empires crumble, but a father's influence can last forever in the memory and character of his family.

It's easy to measure the success of a business venture, but when it comes to fatherhood, success is more difficult to quantify. A father can't keep books and figures on his success with his children. Instead, he can measure his success by the men and women his children grow up to be and by the relationship he has with them.

A successful father inspires and encourages his children.

He motivates them to do their best and to be their best, and as those children grow, they will come to treasure the lessons their father taught them. Many teens think their fathers are too hard on them, and perhaps that is some-times the case, but most fathers simply see their children's potential and don't want them to settle for anything less. A successful father is a role model to his children, an example of hard work, perseverance, and generosity. He teaches his children that money matters, but people matter more.

Most importantly, a successful father is one who lets his children know that he loves them. Whether or not a father can provide a lavish lifestyle for his children is irrelevant. All that matters is that he provides them with what they need—both temporally and emotionally—and what they need most is love. Most fathers know that their success in any given career is meaningless if they fail as a father. A father is successful when his children simply know his is there for them.

Of course, worldly achievement is worth pursuing, but the man who lovingly teaches his children to work hard will always be counted as more successful than the man who makes millions but never makes time for his children. Successful parenting doesn't require perfection. But a man who can be called "Father" by children he loves is already a success.

These quotes voice aspirations of success in fatherhood—the greatest success a man can achieve.

—*Brooke Jorden*

"A truly rich man is one whose children run into his arms when his hands are empty."

—Anonymous

"My dad was my best friend and greatest role model. He was an amazing dad, coach, mentor, soldier, husband, and friend."

—Tiger Woods
American professional golfer

"Sometimes the poorest man leaves his children the richest inheritance."

—Ruth E. Renkel
German writer

"The kind of man who thinks that helping with the dishes is beneath him will also think that helping with the baby is beneath him, and then he certainly is not going to be a very successful father."

—Eleanor Roosevelt
American first lady and wife of Franklin D. Roosevelt

"In order to succeed, your desire for success should be greater than your fear of failure."

—Bill Cosby
American actor and comedian

Being a **father**,
being a FRIEND,
those are the things
that make me feel
SUCCESSFUL.

—William Hurt
American actor

"[Fatherhood] is my most important role. If I fail at this, I fail at everything."

—Mark Wahlberg
American actor

"He went and bought me a guitar, for no apparent reason. I think this was my first personal encounter with music. So what I do now is all my dad's fault."

—Rod Stewart
British singer-songwriter

"Success is to be measured not so much by the position that one has reached in life as by the obstacles which he has overcome."

—Booker T. Washington
American educator, author, and orator

"There is one title I cherish a great deal more than Congressman, and that is the title of Dad."

—J.C. Watts
American politician

"When a man has done his best, has given his all, and in the process supplied the needs of his family and his society, that man has made a habit of succeeding."

—Mack R. Douglas
American author

"Becoming a dad was the proudest moment of my life. Playing football does not even compare."

—Wayne Rooney
English PL footballer (soccer player)

"By profession I am a soldier and take great pride in that fact, but I am prouder, infinitely prouder, to be a father. A soldier destroys in order to build; the father only builds, never destroys. The one has the potentialities of death; the other embodies creation and life. And while the hordes of death are mighty, the battalions of life are mightier still."

—Douglas MacArthur
Reminiscences

"As good as my records are or as proud as I am of the music that I make, I will never create anything a billionth as good as what I'm about to create."

—Michael Bublé
Canadian singer-songwriter, on having a child

"He has achieved success who has worked well, laughed often, and loved much."

—Elbert Hubbard
American writer, artist, and philosopher

Above all,
children need
our unconditional love,
whether they **succeed**
or make **mistakes;** when life is *easy*
and
when life is **tough.**

—Barack Obama
44th US president

47

My prescription for *success*
is based on something
my father always used to tell me:
You should *never try*
to be better than someone else,
but you should *never cease trying*
to be the best you can be.

—John Wooden
American NCAA basketball player and coach

"It's just really making sure I am doing the best job I can do as a dad. I do think that is my number one job."

—Tony Dungy
American NFL football player and coach

"My father was not a failure. After all, he was the father of a president of the United States."

—Harry S. Truman
33rd US president

"Fatherhood is the best thing I ever did. It changes your perspective. You can write a book, you can make a movie, you can paint a painting, but having kids is really the most extraordinary thing I have taken on."

—Brad Pitt
American actor and producer

"Nothing I've ever done has given me more joys and rewards than being a father to my children."

—Bill Cosby
American actor and comedian

"Strive not to be a success, but rather to be of value."

—Albert Einstein
German-born American theoretical physicist

"Being a father has been, without a doubt, my greatest source of achievement, pride, and inspiration. Fatherhood has taught me about unconditional love, reinforced the importance of giving back, and taught me how to be a better person."

—Naveen Jain
Indian entrepreneur and philanthropist

"My father used to say that it's never too late to do anything you wanted to do. And he said, 'You never know what you can accomplish until you try.'"

—Michael Jordan
American NBA basketball player

"I wasn't anything special as a father. But I loved them and they knew it."

—Sammy Davis Jr.
American entertainer

"Of all the titles that I've been privileged to have, Dad has always been the best."

—Ken Norton
American WBC heavyweight boxer

CHARACTER

"It doesn't matter who my father was; it matters who I remember he was."

—Anne Sexton, American poet

Every man has a special set of attributes, a combination of traits that make him who he is. These traits make up what we call character—the thing that defines each individual person. But when he becomes a dad, there is a shift. In many ways he is the same person he has always been; most of the traits stay the same, and he may not even notice that he's changing, but there's something about the transition to fatherhood that changes him forever.

It's subtle at first. One or two bad habits start to dwindle. His better traits get stronger. The worse ones (well, some of them) slowly disappear. Maybe it's the power of the child's presence or the pressure to be a good father, but there's a stronger, more subconscious impetus behind it. A special type of character only comes with being a father, and it comes naturally and slips in unnoticed. It begins with the birth of that first child and the father's realization that his life suddenly means a whole lot more. Now his life means the well-being of his children, his family, and the future of both.

From that moment on, he becomes something greater, and over time he continues to step up and change in ways he never thought possible. He loves more deeply than he ever has before, and is willing to give his life up for his child and the chance to give him or her a better one. He develops a stronger sense of pride—but not the wicked or corrupt kind of pride. It's a pride in his family. A pride in seeing his children grow up to be healthy, strong adults (and maybe in seeing the ways they reflect himself).

But not all aspects of being a dad are as subtle. There are things he consciously gives up, and it's these things that even more firmly strengthen the character of a father. It's the times he stays home with a sick child and gives away his tickets to the big game. The times he's late for a meeting because his little girl skinned her knee. The times he spends hours putting a restless child to bed. The times he starts "boogie-ing down" in the middle of a crowded place, not caring how silly he looks, because his child started dancing and he couldn't help but join in.

Every day, fathers demonstrate the depth of their character. They teach their children that character is the true definition of a person, and they teach that lesson by example.

He's strong. He's heroic. He's wise. He's funny. He's confident. He's family oriented. He's determined. He's flexible. He's patient. He's giving. He's selfless. He's loving. He's Dad.

These quotes represent the strong character that is built and refined in the process of fatherhood.

—*Aven Rose*

"My father was the guy on the block who said 'Hi' to everyone."

—Damon Wayans
American comedian and actor

"A father is a man who expects his son to be as good a man as he meant to be."

—Frank A. Clark
Former American politician

"I'm a good dad; I spend a lot of time with my kids."

—Steve Zahn
American actor and comedian

"Lately all my friends are worried that they're turning into their fathers. I'm worried that I'm not."

—Dan Zevin
American author and humorist

"I like to think my dad was easygoing and kind, and I think some of those things have been passed down. I am like him in a sense of being positive and hopeful. He was compassionate, and I've got a lot of that in me as well."

—Joel Osteen
American televangelist and author

"When I was twenty-something, I asked my father, 'When did you start feeling like a grownup?' His response: 'Never.'"

—Shannon Celebi
American fiction writer

"I was raised by free-spirited people, though my father gave me a very strong work ethic."

—Diane Lane
American actress

"When wealth is lost, nothing is lost; when health is lost, something is lost; when character is lost, all is lost."

—Billy Graham
American minister

"You always hear people saying, 'I hope I'm not turning into my dad,' but I'd be honored if I became half as decent a bloke as he is."

—Johnny Vegas
English actor and comedian

"Character is like a tree and reputation like a shadow. The shadow is what we think of it; the tree is the real thing."

—Abraham Lincoln
16th US president

One of the scary things is that, **when you're a kid,** you look at your **dad** as the man **who has no fear.** When you're an adult, you realize **your father had fear** and that you have it, too

—David Duchovny
American actor, writer, and director

Men should always change diapers.
It's a very rewarding experience.
It's mentally cleansing.
It's like washing dishes,
but imagine if the
      dishes were your kids,
so you really love the dishes.

—Chris Martin
American singer-songwriter

"Be a dad. Don't be 'Mom's assistant.' That's depressing, just waiting for her to write you a list, walk around a store staring at it, calling her from the cereal aisle to make sure you got the right thing. Be a man. Make your own list. Fathers have skills that they never use at home. You run a landscaping business and you can't dress and feed a four-year-old? Take it on. Spend time with your kids and have your own ideas about what they need. It won't take away your manhood; it will give it to you. I did that. I spent more time with my kids. And I found out that I'm a pretty bad father. I make a lot of mistakes and I don't know what I'm doing. But my kids love me. Go figure."

—Louis C.K.
Mexican-American comedian, writer, and actor

"Strength of character means the ability to overcome resentment against others, to hide hurt feelings, and to forgive quickly."

—Lawrence G. Lovasik
American author and missionary

"I love being a dad. I just love it."

—Jerry Seinfeld
American comedian, actor, and producer

"Every day I'm proud to be a dad. When you have kids, there's no such thing as quality time. There's just time. There's no, 'Ooh, this graduation's better than going to the mall.' It's all kind of equal. Changing her diaper and her winning a contest—it's all good."

—Chris Rock
American comedian, actor, and producer

"My dad had a personal style which was very attractive. It was quite reserved and quite elegant, and it was infectious. He liked a good sports jacket and a good pair of trousers, with one hand in his pocket and a cigarette in the other. He couldn't understand why anybody would use bad language in front of a woman or a child. He would get up if a woman came in the room. I find myself doing that sometimes and I sit back down again because they are just going to think I'm weird."

—Bill Nighy
English actor

"Success is not final, failure is not fatal: it is the courage to continue that counts."

—Winston Churchill
British Prime Minister and politician

Noble
fathers
have
noble
children.

—Euripides
Classical Greek tragedian

When you have kids,
it takes the focus off of you.
You forget about what
clothes you're wearing,
or if you went to the gym.
It makes you a better person
if you do it right.

—James Denton Jr.
American actor

"Character is higher than intellect. A great soul will be strong to live as well as think."

—Ralph Waldo Emerson
American Transcendentalist writer

"I hope I am remembered by my children as a good father."

—Orson Scott Card
American novelist and speaker

LEARNING

"One father is more than a hundred schoolmasters."

—George Herbert, Welsh-born English poet and priest

Children are naturally curious about the world around them. From the time children can speak, their questions come in a constant stream: "Why is the sky blue?" "Why do the leaves change colors?" "Why does the moon change shape?" And who better to answer those questions than the all-knowing father?

In a child's eyes, Dad knows everything. He seems ancient and wise; he must be the smartest man in the entire world. Teens begin to suspect that their fathers don't really know anything at all, but when those teens reach adulthood, their perspective shifts again. Although they no longer believe in the total omniscience of their father, they remember all the life lessons that he taught them and the wisdom that he shared with them. They trust his experience. They know that no matter how old they get, they will never be too old to learn from their father.

Every father knows that the most valuable and important learning happens outside of the classroom. A father is the most influential teacher because he teaches by quiet example and wise words. Dad's lessons are not about algebra or chemistry—although he'll help with homework when he can and teach his children the importance of education. A father's lessons are more substantial and lasting. He will teach his sons how to be men and teach his daughters how they should be treated. He will encourage his children to ask questions and make observations. He will inspire his children to try their hardest and be their best.

Ironically, fatherhood teaches the father as much as it teaches the child. When a father takes the time to listen, he'll be amazed by the simple wisdom of his children. Fathers make mistakes like everyone else, and children will learn as much from their father's mistakes as they do from his lessons. So, as new fathers begin their journey of parenthood, they need not fear ineptitude or failure. No matter how many parenting books a man reads, no matter how many parenting seminars he attends, nothing can fully prepare him for the experience of being a father. But that doesn't matter. Fatherhood is a learning process with on-the-job training, and learning to be a good father usually teaches that father to be a better man, too.

These quotes describe the lessons that fathers learn and the lessons they teach to their children.

—*Brooke Jorden*

"Before I got married. I had six theories about bringing up children; now I have six children, and no theories."

—John Wilmot
English poet and 2nd Earl of Rochester

"My father was my teacher. But most importantly, he was a great dad. "

—Beau Bridges
American actor and director

"Fathers, like mothers, are not born. Men grow into fathers, and fathering is a very important stage in their development."

—David Gottesman
American businessman and billionaire

"My dad always taught me to never be satisfied, to want more and know that what is done is done."

—Thierry Henry
French MLS footballer (soccer player)

"The nature of impending fatherhood is that you are doing something that you're unqualified to do, and then you become qualified by doing it."

—John Green
American writer and educator

Education begins at home, and I applaud the parents who recognize that they— not someone else— must take responsibility to assure that their children are well educated.

—Ernest Istook
American politician

"It was my dad who encouraged me to question everything, to forge my own path, to think, to read. I always felt it was my right to question everything."

—Dan Stevens
English actor

"Children are educated by what the grown-up is and not by his talk."

—Carl Jung
Swiss psychiatrist and theorist

"I never saw my dad cry. My son saw me cry. My dad never told me he loved me, and consequently I told Scott I loved him every other minute. The point is, I'll make less mistakes than my dad, my sons hopefully will make less mistakes than me, and their sons will make less mistakes than their dads."

—James Caan
American actor

"My father was a person who never lied to me. If I had a question, he answered it. I knew a lot of things at a young age because I was intrigued."

—Nick Cannon
American comedian, rapper, and TV personality

"The things that have been most valuable to me I did not learn in school."

—Will Smith
American actor, producer, and rapper

"If a son is uneducated, his father is to blame."

—Chinese proverb

"These guys who fear becoming fathers don't understand that fathering is not something perfect men do, but something that perfects the man. The end product of child-raising is not the child but the parent."

—Frank Pittman
Man Enough

"Nothing in the world is more dangerous than sincere ignorance and conscientious stupidity."

—Martin Luther King Jr.
American clergyman and civil rights activist

"While we teach and inspire our children, it's they who truly teach and inspire us. Every day."

—Vicki Reece
American CEO and activist

The father who does
not teach his son
his duties
is equally guilty
with the son
who neglects
them.

—Confucius
Chinese teacher and philosopher

Dad **taught** me
everything I know.
Unfortunately,
he **didn't teach** me
everything **he knows.**

—Al Unser
American racecar driver

"Live as if you were to die tomorrow. Learn as if you were to live forever."

—Mahatma Gandhi
Indian civil rights activist

"The most challenging part of being a dad is self-restraint. So often your instinct is to teach and tell. I am constantly reminding myself to listen to them."

—Michael Chiklis
American actor, director, and producer

"Learning is the beginning of wealth. Learning is the beginning of health. Learning is the beginning of spirituality. Searching and learning is where the miracle process all begins."

—Jim Rohn
American entrepreneur, author, and motivational speaker

"Fathers in today's modern families can be so many things."

—Oliver Hudson
American actor

"Don't limit a child to your own learning, for he was born in another time."

—Rabindranath Tagore
Bengali author and musician

"The only way we really learn is by figuring it out as we go along, and even then it changes on us every day, so we're always improvising, which is a fancy way of saying that we're doing things we technically don't know how to do."

—Ben Fountain
American fiction writer

"If I am through learning, I am through."

—John Wooden
American NCAA basketball player and coach

WISDOM AND JUDGMENT

"The words that a father speaks to his children in the privacy of home are not heard by the world, but, as in whispering-galleries, they are clearly heard at the end and by posterity."

—Jean Paul Richter, German Romantic writer

Dad knows about cars. He knows about fishing. He knows about politics and history and will probably tell you all about it. But more importantly, Dad always knows what to do, and when we come to him for advice, we're going to get what we asked for and then some. Despite the stories that we know we'll hear, the ones about a childhood lacking in technology and full of snowy weather, we still turn to our fathers for insight when the going gets tough. That fatherly wisdom seems to come naturally, but we know that the wisdom a father imparts to his children has been earned in the blood, sweat, tears, and years of his own experience.

A father's wisdom is invaluable. When we lose a father or father-figure, we will miss the laughs and the barbeques, but what we'll miss most is the free-flowing stream of advice—even if we don't always appreciate it now. The wise counsel of a father is always given in love, so it should never be taken too lightly.

Ironically, perhaps the most difficult part of fatherhood is finding out that no father is all-knowing. Sometimes a father's judgment can be clouded or misguided. In such instances, and whenever a father has an open mind and a loving heart, he can learn from the wisdom of his children. And fathers should be grateful for those lessons. However, as the job description implies, being a father often means that, even when he feels inadequate, his children need the wisdom he has acquired, informed by his love for and personal knowledge of each individual child, to guide them through the troubles that are sure to come in childhood, adolescence, and beyond.

Fatherhood requires wisdom grounded in experience and time; it demands judgment grounded in foresight and love. A father's advice comes from the heart, with his children's best interests in mind. Even when a father has to dole out punishments, he does so in love, and even if his children don't understand his judgments when he gives them, they come to accept his wisdom later and appreciate his efforts to guide them.

So whether he is waxing wise or simply wise-cracking, the next time Dad says, "You know, when I was a kid . . . " perhaps we ought to listen and see what wisdom we can glean.

These quotes represent the wisdom of generations of fathers who passed their knowledge on to the children they love.

—*Brooke Jorden*

"My dad is such a good man. You know how when you are a child you think your dad is invincible? Well, I still think that—he is so wise, and everything I do I ask my dad's advice about first."

—Leona Lewis
British singer-songwriter

"I believe that what we become depends on what our fathers teach us at odd moments, when they aren't trying to teach us. We are formed by little scraps of wisdom."

—Umberto Eco
Foucault's Pendulum

"My father said, 'Politics asks the question: Is it expedient? Vanity asks: Is it popular? But conscience asks: Is it right?'"

—Dexter Scott King
Son of civil rights activist Martin Luther King Jr.

"To be satisfied with a little, is the greatest wisdom; and he that increaseth his riches, increaseth his cares; but a contented mind is a hidden treasure, and trouble findeth it not."

—Akhenaten
Egyptian pharaoh

"My father, he was like the rock, the guy you went to with every problem."

—Gwyneth Paltrow
American actress and singer

"Wisdom, compassion, and courage are the three universally recognized moral qualities of men."

—Confucius
Chinese teacher and philosopher

"I think I know how to raise a kid. You just play catch with 'em. You just talk about life, and you distract them by throwing the ball. They don't even notice that you're filling up their heads with your theories."

—Bill Burr
American comedian and actor

"Some folks are wise, and some are otherwise."

—Tobias Smollett
Scottish poet and author

"My dad always said, 'Champ, the measure of a man is not how often he is knocked down, but how quickly he gets up.'"

—Joe Biden
American vice president

My father always told me,
"Find a job you *love*
and you'll never have to
work a day in your *life*."

—Jim Fox
American NHL hockey player

A good father needs **infinite patience,** boundless enthusiasm, **kindness,** the ability to score a goal, **take a wicket,** and hit a winning serve, **and the strength to say "no"** every now and again.

—Piers Morgan
British journalist and TV host

"But my father was also the one who told me I needed to clean up my mouth or I'd never find a man. What's very important to him is manners. Show up on time. Always send thank-you letters. He is one of the more thoughtful humans I've ever met. He's a great man and a very good dad."

—Zosia Mamet
American actress

"Honesty is the first chapter in the book of wisdom."

—Thomas Jefferson
3rd US president

"The only true wisdom is in knowing you know nothing."

—Socrates
Classical Greek philosopher

"My dad encouraged us to fail. Growing up, he would ask us what we failed at that week. If we didn't have something, he would be disappointed. It changed my mindset at an early age that failure is not the outcome; failure is not trying. Don't be afraid to fail."

—Sara Blakely
American business woman and billionaire

"To make no mistakes is not in the power of man; but from their errors and mistakes the wise and good learn wisdom for the future."

—Plutarch
Greek historian and essayist

"A man must be big enough to admit his mistakes, smart enough to profit from them, and strong enough to correct them."

—John C. Maxwell
Christian author and pastor

"My dad always said, 'Don't worry what people think, because you can't change it.'"

—Daisy Donovan
English TV presenter, actress, and writer

"Counsel woven into the fabric of real life is wisdom."

—Walter Benjamin
German literary critic and philosopher

"I have found the best way to give advice to your children is to find out what they want and then advise them to do it."

—Harry S. Truman
33rd US president

A loving heart is the truest wisdom.

—Charles Dickens
English writer and social critic

"**Principles are the most important thing to me. One of the things I think my dad taught me was there are people who accept the world they live in and there are people who change the world they live in. I don't accept my circumstances.**"

—Ken Buck
American politician and district attorney

LEADERSHIP AND ROLE MODELS

"My father didn't tell me how to live; he lived, and let me watch him do it."

—Clarence B. Kelland, American writer

A dad is always there to lead his children—whether they want him to or not. It's in his job description: "Drag your children to things they don't want to go to, embarrass them in public, and teach them things they never wanted to learn." OK, maybe that's just a teenager's interpretation of it.

But is it that interpretation so far off? One of a father's biggest responsibilities is to be a role model for his children. It is his job to be someone they can look up to and aspire to imitate, and he has a responsibility to raise his children in a way that makes it possible for them to do so. He drags his children to boring events because the event is for a good cause, because the event will help them learn something, or because attending the event will show support to someone they love. Each event teaches them something new about themselves, whether that be something big—like a new passion in life—or something small—like finding out that they have a higher tolerance for "boring" than they previously believed.

Embarrassing children in public teaches them self-confidence. Children need a role model to teach them that it doesn't matter what other people think as as long as they are having fun and being true to themselves. (Parents, think about how great this justification is!)

Fathers might talk their children's ears off about random moments in history or antique furniture or their high school lives or other things kids couldn't care less about, but the children always come away with something new. And who doesn't love the rare moments when an obscure question comes up in conversation and you can say "I know the answer!"? Especially when it's because of your dad. Besides, how often does Dad patiently listen to endless chatter about Justin Beiber or the new video game about to come out or the cute guy in geometry class or how mad you are at your coach. The list goes on and on.

Then there are the random moments that make us all proud to call our father "Dad." That time you crashed his car while learning how to drive and his first concern wasn't checking the car, but making sure you got back behind the wheel so it didn't scare you. The way his co-workers respect him. The times he was willing to jump in the car in the middle of the night to come save you from a bad situation. The busy days when he kept his cool, no matter how frustrated he got. The way he's able to talk to anyone and everyone. The times when you see how hard he works to keep everyone in his family happy, safe, and together. The way he believes in you, no matter what.

In short, dads are pretty amazing. We may not all want to be just like our old man, but no matter our age, we sure look to our fathers to show us how to live, and most of them are pretty darn good at showing us how.

These quotes examine the ways in which fathers accept and develop their leadership roles.

—*Aven Rose*

Do I want to be a *hero* to my son?
No.
I would like to be a
very real human being.
That's hard enough.

—Robert Downey Jr.
American actor and producer

"As a dad, you are the Vice President of the executive branch of parenting. It doesn't matter what your personality is like, you will always be Al Gore to your wife's Bill Clinton. She feels the pain and you are the annoying nerd telling them to turn off the lights."

—Jim Gaffigan
American comedian and author

"You know, no matter what I am or what I do for a living, I'm still, you know, the husband and the dad and the protector of the house, and I have to be conscientious about that."

—Richie Sambora
American rock guitarist and singer-songwriter

"A man's children and his garden both reflect the amount of weeding done during the growing season."

—Anonymous

"You hate to say things that will upset your kids, but then sometimes you have to because you can't let them run around wild."

—Ozzy Osbourne
English rock vocalist, songwriter, and TV personality

"Becoming a dad means you have to be a role model for your son and be someone he can look up to."

—Wayne Rooney
English PL footballer (soccer player)

"My dad was my biggest supporter. He never put pressure on me."

—Bobby Orr
Canadian NHL hockey player

"Dads are most ordinary men turned by love into heroes, adventurers, storytellers, singers of songs."

—Pam Brown
Australian poet

"All fathers . . . are invisible in daytime; daytime is ruled by mothers. But fathers come out at night. Darkness brings home fathers, with their real, unspeakable power. There is more to them than meets the eye."

—Margaret Atwood
Cat's Eye

"Two of my biggest heroes were my father and John Wayne."

—Johnny Ramone
American guitarist and songwriter

A father must lead his children;

but first he must learn to follow.

He must laugh with them but remember the ache of childhood tears.

He must hold the past with one hand and reach to the future with the other so there can be no generation gap in family love.

—June Masters Bacher
American author

89

I talk and talk and talk,
and I haven't taught people
in fifty years
what my father
taught by example
in one week.

—Mario Cuomo
Former American politician

"I deal with my sons like young men. If they have a problem with something, they come to me. I am the type of dad that will drop everything I am doing for them, and always tell them to talk to me about it."

—Tracy Morgan
American actor and comedian

"When I was a kid, my father told me every day, 'You're the most wonderful boy in the world, and you can do anything you want to.'"

—Jan Hutchins
American journalist, producer, and media consultant

"A good father is one of the most unsung, unpraised, unnoticed, and yet one of the most valuable assets in our society."

—Billy Graham
American minister

"Leading a family is the hardest job a man can ever have."

—Dave Ramsey
American author, radio host, and TV personality

"My daddy, he was somewhere between God and John Wayne."

—Hank Williams Jr.
American country music singer-songwriter

"My father gave me the greatest gift anyone could give another person: he believed in me."

—Jim Valvano
American NCAA basketball coach and broadcaster

"Then, I thought Dad was teaching me to ride a bike without training wheels; now, I know he was showing me how to stand on my own two feet."

—Jim Wilcox
American artist

"Why are dads like this? From the moment you were born, they have known their roles—to be a strong force in your life. That's why they must remain larger than you, smarter than you, and give you someone to emulate—if they do it right."

—Erma Bombeck
American author and humorist

"Every family needs three things from a father: provision, protection, and direction. How well a man handles these three responsibilities is a test of his manhood."

—Philip Lancaster
American author and editor

Hail Mary passes
        don't work in fatherhood.
Fathering is all about a dad
moving the ball forward
in his relationship with his child,
one yard at a time,
        day in and day out.

—Mark Merrill
All Pro Dad

**Dad, you're someone
to look up to . . .
no matter how
tall I've grown.**

—Anonymous

"My heroes are and were my parents. I can't see having anyone else as my heroes."

—Michael Jordan
American NBA basketball player

"Your job [as dad] is not that of a general contractor . . . Your job is that of CEO in your home."

—Mark Merrill
All Pro Dad

"Every father should remember that one day his son will follow his example, not his advice."

—Charles F. Kettering
American inventor, engineer, and businessman

FATHERS AND DAUGHTERS

"To a father growing old, nothing is dearer than a daughter."

—Euripides, classical Greek tragedian

Of all the relationships in the world, few are as special as that of a father and his daughter. However much he loves his wife, from the day his daughter is born, she shows him a new way to love. While her mother rests, he holds the infant in his arms and realizes that a part of him has suddenly been filled—a part he didn't know was empty until that very moment. He swears to protect her, to love her in any way possible. He knows he will always be happiest with his daughter in his arms.

He lets her pick her own outfit for her very first day of kindergarten and holds in his laughter when she proudly shows him her outfit, complete with a giant hat, polka dot dress, striped leggings, and the "very special" plastic Cinderella heels she wore for Halloween. He marches her to school, holding his head just as high as hers, ready to argue with and deflect anyone who tries to tell her she looks anything but perfect.

He learns to braid her hair (perhaps slowly and clumsily) when her mother can't, and talks to her about her latest movie obsession or the kids at school or whatever else is on her mind. He helps her practice for ballet class, even though he has no idea what he's doing, and teaches her to waltz to the soundtrack of her favorite princess movie—the one they have seen together at least a thousand times. His little girl sings along to the soundtrack, sure that she looks and sounds just as beautiful as the princess, and no matter what, in his eyes, she's better.

He loves her through her awkward transition years, when she is no longer a little girl, but not yet an adult, or even a teenager. And though he may grimace at the idea of his little girl becoming a woman (and the things that come with it), he is there for her every step of the way. He is there for her when she's in tears over her first heartbreak, big or small, to reassure her that, though men are pigs (especially the ones that make her cry), someday she will find one who will transform into a prince, just for her. And she believes him, because he has filled that role since the day she was born.

He teaches her right from wrong, hopes she chooses the former, and struggles through her punishments as much as she does when she makes mistakes. But no matter what, he makes sure that she knows that however angry they get, and however grown up and independent she becomes, she always has a place with him.

The first time she leaves the house is the hardest and proudest day for both of them, but he lets her go, knowing that he has taught her how to find her way in the world. And even though she will never say it aloud, he has taught her what to look for in a man, how much she deserves to be loved, and to never settle for less. He supports her through every frantic phone call and every financial crisis (even the ones that come at 3:00 a.m.) without complaint, because these are proof that no matter how old she gets, she will always need her dad.

Then, before he knows it, she's in his arms again, dressed in white, with another man's last name, and her face is more radiant than it's ever been before. He remembers every time she crawled into his lap as a child, the first time he taught her how to change a tire (and the second, and the third), every time she looked at him like he was flawless—like he was her hero. And he knows that although she's found a new prince, a part of her will always belong to him. She will always be his little girl.

These quotes represent the special, unbreakable bond between fathers and their daughters.

—*Aven Rose*

"Certain is it that there is no kind of affection so purely angelic as of a father to a daughter. In love to our wives, there is desire; to our sons, ambition; but to our daughters, there is something which there are no words to express."

—Joseph Addison
English essayist, poet, and politician

"Old as she was, she still missed her daddy sometimes."

—Gloria Naylor
American novelist and educator

"To be the father of growing daughters is to understand something of what Yeats evokes with his imperishable phrase 'terrible beauty.' Nothing can make one so happily exhilarated or so frightened: it's a solid lesson in the limitations of self to realize that your heart is running around inside someone else's body. It also makes me quite astonishingly calm at the thought of death: I know whom I would die to protect, and I also understand that nobody but a lugubrious serf can possibly wish for a father who never goes away."

—Christopher Hitchens
Hitch-22: A Memoir

To her,
the name **of father**
was another name **for**
love**.**

—Fanny Fern
American columnist and author

The father of a daughter
is nothing but a
high-class hostage.
A father turns a stony face
to his sons,
berates them,
shakes his antlers,
paws the ground,
snorts,
runs them off into the underbrush,
but when his daughter
puts her arm over his shoulder
and says,
"Daddy, I need to ask you something,"
he is a
pat of butter
in a hot frying pan.

—Garrison Keillor
American author, humorist, and radio personality

"It is admirable for a man to take his son fishing, but there is a special place in heaven for the father who takes his daughter shopping."

—John Sinor
American author and columnist

"Look, I've got incredible pride for my family. I've absolutely fallen into that cliché of a dad who could just happily talk about my daughter endlessly."

—Christian Bale
English actor

"How does a father demonstrate commitment to his daughter? By loving her when she is the most unlovable. Unconditional love reflects commitment— 'I will always love you. No matter what.'"

—Tim Smith
English singer-songwriter and poet

"Any astronomer can predict with absolute accuracy just where every star in the universe will be at 11:30 tonight. He can make no such prediction about his teenage daughter."

—James T. Adams
American writer and historian

"A wedding is for daughters and fathers. The mothers all dress up, trying to look like young women. But a wedding is for a father and daughter. They stop being married to each other on that day."

—Sarah Ruhl
Eurydice

"My dad's contentment is all that matters to me. When he's laughing, I'm laughing. When he's happy, I'm happy. I would give up my soul for him. To me, nothing else but his happiness matters."

—Rebecah McManus
Colliding Worlds

"I think a dad has to make his daughter feel that he's genuinely interested in what she's going through."

—Harry Connick Jr.
American singer, composer, and actor

"My father died many years ago, and yet when something special happens to me, I talk to him secretly not really knowing whether he hears, but it makes me feel better to half believe it."

—Natasha Josefowitz
American author and columnist

There's something like a line of gold thread running through a **man's words** when he talks to his daughter, **and gradually** over the years it gets to be long enough for you to pick up in your hands and weave into a cloth that feels like **love itself.**

—John Gregory Brown
Decorations in a Ruined Cemetery

You fathers will *understand*.
You have a little girl.
She *looks up* to you.
You're her ORACLE.
You're her hero.
And then the day comes
when she gets her first permanent wave
and goes to her first real party,
and from that day on,
you're in a
constant state of panic.

—Stanley T. Banks
from *The Father of the Bride* (1991)

"I've made it my business to observe fathers and daughters. And I've seen some incredible, beautiful things. Like the little girl who's not very cute—her teeth are funny, and her hair doesn't grow right, and she's got on thick glasses—but her father holds her hand and walks with her like she's a tiny angel that no one can touch. He gives her the best gift a woman can get in this world: protection. And the little girl learns to trust the man in her life. And all the things that the world expects from women—to be beautiful, to soothe the troubled spirit, heal the sick, care for the dying, send the greeting card, bake the cake—all of those things become the way we pay the father back for protecting us."

—Adriana Trigiani
Big Stone Gap

"I look at my little girl and I wonder what she's going to be and what she's going to do and what is it that leads girls certain directions in life. I think a lot of that goes back to what kind of father they had, and so it makes me want to be the best dad I can possibly be."

—Jake Owen
American country music artist

"One of the greatest things about daughters is how they adored you when they were little; how they rushed into your arms with electric delight and demanded that you watch everything they do and listen to everything they say. Those memories will help you through less joyous times when their adoration is replaced by embarrassment or annoyance, and they don't want you to see what they are doing or hear what they are saying. And yet, you will adore your daughter every day of her life, hoping to be valued again, but realizing how fortunate you were even if you only get what you already got."

—Michael Josephson
American author and ethicist

"A father is always making his baby into a little woman. And when she is a woman, he turns her back again."

—Enid Bagnold
British author and playwright

"I thought I would be inspired to have all these new feelings to talk about, but I really just want to hang out with my daughter."

—Jay-Z
American rapper and record producer

"I figure if I kill the first one, word will get out."

—Charles Barkley
NBA basketball player and analyst

"It's a great joy, but no test of love or commitment to take your son to a ball game. You really prove your credentials as a good dad when you are willing to take your daughter shopping—more than once."

—Michael Josephson
American author and ethicist

FATHERS IN FILM AND MEDIA

"Then a thought popped into my head, kids, the same thought that will pop into your heads the first time you see your best friend holding their baby: That guy's a dad!"

—Ted Mosby, *How I Met Your Mother* (2012)

Fathers in the media—some are heroes, some are villains. From Mr. Incredible to Darth Vader, the portrayals of fathers in film and media range to every extreme. Some fathers have an evident darker side, others neglect their children, and still others are positive role models (think Crush from *Finding Nemo* (2003))—the types of fathers are endless. The media has produced some of the most lovable and some of the most despicable fathers—and we can learn something from each of them.

Today, our culture and perception of life is based heavily on the media, and often life begins to imitate art. Ty Burrell, the American actor best known for his fatherly role in ABC's hit comedy *Modern Family*, put it this way: "I think once I fail enough as a dad, I'll be looking for help wherever I can get it. I just need enough time to screw things up, and then I'll be looking to TV dads for advice." All joking aside, our views of fatherhood often come from seeing the good, the bad, and the ugly styles of parenting in film and other mediums.

In film, songs, and popular literature, fathers rarely measure up to the ideal. Their weaknesses range from incompetence to obliviousness to indifference. Some dominate their homes like frightful tyrants, while others are absent, invisible, or weak. And yet, there are many fathers—in movies and songs, especially—who inspire us with their love and courage, despite their imperfections. They learn from their mistakes and always try to be the best father they can be.

Often in films, fathers take a transformative journey—whether literal or metaphorical—that turns them into better dads. Many a father on the big screen comes to realize what really matters in his life—his relationship with his family. Many, like Mr. Banks in *Mary Poppins* (1964), decide that money and position mean nothing if you can't spend time simply flying a kite with your children. Others, like Peter Banning in *Hook* (1991), discover that fatherhood, not success, is their happiest thought. And the best fathers, like Christopher Gardner in *The Pursuit of Happyness* (2006), will go to any lengths to make certain that their children have a comfortable life and a bright future, but at the end of the day, they know that the most important thing a father can give his children is love.

These quotes—taken from movies, TV shows, and songs—cover the wide range of fathers and fathering styles portrayed by the media.

—Brooke Jorden and Emily Smith

Rufio: Do you know what I wish?

Peter Pan / Banning: What?

Rufio: I wish I had a dad ... like you.

—*Hook* (1991)

"You just have to decide what kind of man you want to grow up to be, Clark. Whoever that man is, he's going to change the world."

—Jonathan Kent
Man of Steel (2013)

"Yes, you wish and you dream with all your little heart. But you remember, Tiana, that that old star can only take you part of the way. You gotta help along with some hard work of your own, and then, yeah, you can do anything you set your mind to. Just promise your daddy one thing: you'll never, ever lose sight of what's really important, OK?"

—Tiana's father
The Princess and the Frog (2009)

"Fine work, my boy! You've done it. You're a true hero ... For a hero isn't measured by the size of his strength, but by the strength of his heart."

—Zeus
Hercules (1997)

"Dad, I may not be the best, but I come to believe that I got it in me to be somebody in this world. And it's not because I'm so different from you, either. It's because I'm the same. I mean, I can be just as hard-headed, and just as tough. I only hope I can be as good a man as you."

—Homer Hickam
October Sky (1999)

"In regards to my behavior, I can only plead insanity, because ever since my children were born, the moment I looked at them, I was crazy about them. And once I held them, I was hooked. I'm addicted to my children, sir. I love them with all my heart, and the idea of someone telling me I can't be with them, I can't see them every day . . . it's like someone saying I can't have air. I can't live without air, and I can't live without them. Listen, I would do anything. I just want to be with them. You know I need that, sir. We have a history. And I just—they mean everything to me, and they need me as much as I need them. So please, don't take my kids away from me."

—Daniel Hillard
Mrs. Doubtfire (1993)

I don't care how poor a man is;
if he has FAMILY,
he's RICH.

—Colonel Potter
M*A*S*H (1981)

Every dad is entitled to one
hideous shirt
and
one **horrible** sweater.
It's part of the
Dad Code.

—Tom Baker
Cheaper by the Dozen 2 (2005)

"A man who doesn't spend time with his family can never be a real man."

—Don Vito Corleone
The Godfather (1972)

Mr. Incredible: [Everyone is trapped in Syndrome's containment unit] I'm sorry. I've been a lousy father, blind to what I have, so obsessed with being undervalued that I undervalued all of you.

[While Bob is talking, Violet frees herself using her force field]

Dash: Uh, dad . . .

Elastigirl: Shh, don't interrupt.

Mr. Incredible: So caught up in the past that I . . . You are my greatest adventure, and I almost missed it. I swear that if we get out of this safely, I will . . .

Violet: [At the control panel] Well, I think dad has made some excellent progress today, but I think it's time we wind down now.

—*The Incredibles* (2004)

"You yell at my kid like that again, I'm knockin' you out!"

—Jack Butler
Mr. Mom (1983)

"There will always be a few people who have the courage to love what is untamed inside us. One of those men is my father."

—Katie McLoughlin
Flicka (2006)

"What's a dad for, dad?

Taught me how to stand, dad.

Took me by the hand

And you showed me how to be a bigger man, dad.

Listen when you talk, dad.

Follow where you walk, dad.

And you know that I will always do the best I can."

—Yellowcard
"Life of a Salesman"

"The first time you hear the word 'Daddy,' I don't care who you are, your heart just melts."

—Cab driver
Three Men and a Baby (1987)

"Dads make the best friends. That's why dogs are always hanging out with them."

—Cliff Huxtable
The Cosby Show (1985)

That's what fathers do . . . they yell and they barbecue. That's what separates them from the apes.

—Dorothy Zbornak
Golden Girls

Only a real man can raise his children.

—Jason Styles
Boyz N the Hood (1991)

"I don't know who you are. I don't know what you want. If you are looking for ransom, I can tell you I don't have money. But what I do have are a very particular set of skills, skills I have acquired over a very long career. Skills that make me a nightmare for people like you. If you let my daughter go now, that'll be the end of it. I will not look for you; I will not pursue you. But if you don't, I will look for you, I will find you, and I will kill you."

—Bryan Mills
Taken (2008)

"No. I am your father . . . Search your feelings. You know it to be true."

—Darth Vader
Star Wars Episode IV: A New Hope (1977)

Christopher Gardner: Hey. Don't ever let somebody tell you you can't do something. Not even me. All right?

Christopher Jr.: All right.

Christopher Gardner: You got a dream, you gotta protect it. People can't do somethin' themselves, they wanna tell you you can't do it. If you want somethin', go get it. Period.

—*The Pursuit of Happyness* (2006)

"The older I get

The more I can see

How much he loved my mother and my brother and me,

And he did the best that he could.

And I only hope when I have my own family

That everyday I see

A little more of my father in me."

—Keith Urban
"Song for Dad"

"As a dad, you're terrific. As a husband, you're more like a traffic cop."

—Annabel Andrews
Freaky Friday (1976)

Squirt: Whoa! That was so cool! Hey, Dad! Did you see that? Did you see me? Did you see what I did?

Crush: You so totally rock, Squirt. Gimme some fin. Noggin.

Both: Dude.

—*Finding Nemo* (2003)

"You have forgotten who you are and so have forgotten me. Look inside yourself, Simba. You are more than what you have become. You must take your place in the circle of life . . . Remember who you are. You are my son and the one true king. Remember who you are."

—Mufasa
The Lion King (1994)

About Familius

Welcome to a place where mothers are celebrated, not compared. Where heart is at the center of our families, and family at the center of our homes. Where boo boos are still kissed, cake beaters are still licked, and mistakes are still okay. Welcome to a place where books—and family—are beautiful. Familius: a book publisher dedicated to helping families be happy.

Visit Our Website: www.familius.com

Our website is a different kind of place. Get inspired, read articles, discover books, watch videos, connect with our family experts, download books and apps and audiobooks, and along the way, discover how values and happy family life go together.

Join Our Family

There are lots of ways to connect with us! Subscribe to our newsletters at www.familius.com to receive uplifting daily inspiration, essays from our Pater Familius, a free ebook every month, and the first word on special discounts and Familius news.

Become an Expert

Familius authors and other established writers interested in helping families be happy are invited to join our family and contribute online content. If you have something important to say on the family, join our expert community by applying at:

www.familius.com/apply-to-become-a-familius-expert

Get Bulk Discounts

If you feel a few friends and family might benefit from what you've read, let us know and we'll be happy to provide you with quantity discounts. Simply email us at specialorders@familius.com.

Website: www.familius.com

Facebook: www.facebook.com/paterfamilius

Twitter: @familiustalk, @paterfamilius1

Pinterest: www.pinterest.com/familius

The most important work

you ever do will be within the

walls of your own home.

SUSTAINABLE
FORESTRY
INITIATIVE
SFI-01156

CPSIA information can be obtained at www.ICGtesting.com
Printed in the USA
BVOW08s2043130314

347631BV00001B/2/P